D0708085

A QUICKENING

Published in 2019 by
Muddy Pearl, Edinburgh, Scotland.
www.muddypearl.com
books@muddypearl.com

© Rosemary Hector 2019
Illustrations © Kelsey Johnston 2019
Rosemary Hector has asserted her right under the Copyright,
Designs and Patents Act 1988 to be identified as the author of this work.

British Library Cataloguing in Publication Data
A catalogue record for this book is available from the British Library
ISBN 978-1-910012-63-5
Typeset in Minion by Revo Creative Ltd, Lancaster
Cover design by Revo Creative Ltd, Lancaster.
Cover illustration by Kelsey Johnston
Printed by Livonia, Latvia

Textures copyright Shutterstock: 205426069, 205426075, 219154477,
289827458, 424974826, 554421208, 668018377, 1010344504, 1419661274

A QUICKENING

ROSEMARY HECTOR

Muddy
Pearl

Contents

Introduction

Shortly after Muddy Pearl invited me to write some pieces around the Christmas story, we went to a remote part of southern Italy to look after a house belonging to a friend. It was Easter. The Holy Week pageants in the local hill town, the landscape and climate made it easy to imagine the context into which Jesus was born.

Some of these pieces were written in that valley in the Gargano, where the noonday sun is fierce, the nights bitterly cold, where olives grew and goats – rather than sheep – roamed freely, overseen by a young herdsman who slept under the trees.

I was challenged as I reread the story of Christmas as presented in the Bible. Was there corroborating evidence that the events actually happened? I read. I attended a school of theology. I asked theologians. The story of how the Bible has been compiled is remarkable. Composed of fragments from a variety of sources, the Scriptures are astonishingly consistent. My first piece reflects on the nature of where this story came from, using a literary form called the 'fragment'.

The story, of course, does not start with the birth of Jesus. I had to consider the prophecies in the Old Testament. After many false starts, I wrote about only one prophesy, in Isaiah, where I felt his observations about the society in which he lived echoed our very modern despair. Equally, I had always considered the genealogies a little dull, but careful rereading and research suggests the writing of these had a purpose, and some pieces in this collection reflect this.

Israel at the time of the birth of Jesus was occupied territory and the Roman senator stationed in this part of the Empire, Herod, was known for his viciousness. His life and his tyrannies are well documented. Head counts, frequent requests for people to register and swear allegiance, and massacres are common tools of tyranny and many such events are in the historical records from that time.

Dreams and songs continue to be part of the Middle-Eastern culture. To the western mind this is very mysterious. The Magi, too, are an exotic element of the story. They were from a foreign culture and nowhere else in the Bible are their trio of gifts, gold, frankincense and myrrh mentioned. How different from the shepherds who brought nothing but their fear and respect for what they had seen. Responding to these different visitors and to the prophets who met Jesus demanded different forms, different words.

The story of a birth is the most human of all stories. That is the simplicity and yet also the mystery of this story. Christians believe that God chose to enter space and time and became a baby. The story echoes the nature of faith; there are gaps, there are moments of doubt. I trust these pieces provide scope for reflection, and provoke us to go back to the narratives recorded in the Bible as we consider this age-old story.

Narrative I

some words on Bethlehem   the rest   lost

(Fire. Mildew; careless storage after rain.)

a voice crying   in the wilderness

                            praise poems

songs to God   (Copied by monks.)

there are scrolls

in jars

dusty artefacts from digs

findings   (Some nibbled by mice.)

fragments   (that scholars

pieced as a miracle of consistency   a story

information woven)   warp of love

a weft

of faith

Lament

... oh i cry for our country   a bank with no money
a shop with nothing to sell   a sandpit not safe for play
because of litter and needles and dog shit
oh i weep bitter tears for our country ...

Isaiah's metaphors were for different times; he wrote
of neglected vineyards, deserts, burning straw, as he wept
for Israel, God's lovely nation. It was the same observation
as today; a failure of justice. Rightness offended.

A prophet's lament is not personal, but mirrors
things as they are. It speaks to those in power,
nor does it offer an answer, provide a neat narrative
with a rhyming conclusion. The call is to consider, return.

Say 'sorry' and attempt to restore all that is broken.
Yet within his descriptions of darkness and woe a small voice
slips in; light. There will be a child. Named 'God with us'.
With us, in all our metaphors. In all our times.

Messenger

A prophet would be too obvious

and the wrong type to visit.

Prone to halitosis and poor sight,

whiskery, too terrifying for a girl

who has never had attention –

been the focus of any gathering.

Prophets speak to nations, not girls.

Imagine the gossip if one turned up.

No, it has to be one of the specials

from here, not with earth-encrusted feet.

Sweet-breathed, yes, with a smile,

of indeterminate age, neutral dress,

a little fluttery, perhaps, but personal,

straight-from-God. Yes, Gabriel.

The Annunciation

No blue dress, golden crown,

stairs leading the eye

to an artful chink of sky.

No lily in its vase,

superfluity of feathers, for

Gabriel was familiar, in sandals.

Only a reasonable query,

quashed with the extraordinary.

A breathless 'yes'.

Joseph

We assume her explanation

had left Joseph at the edge

of trust. Had she doubts too?

(A time-of-the-month fantasy?)

The stranger's word assured him.

A gifted messenger, persuasive

for God's face-to-face. Boy talk.

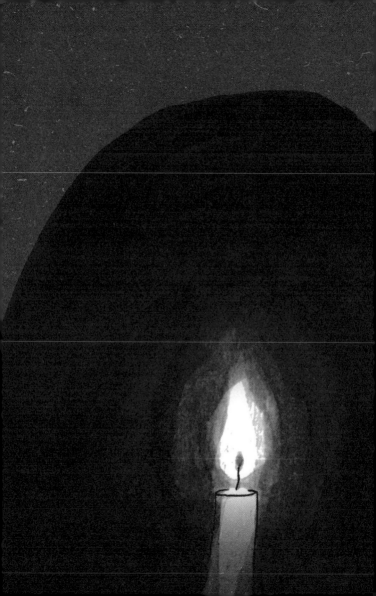

If

If
she's right
we're found.

If
God lit
the flame
that burned
then light
has won
and God
has come.

If
she's right
then God
has come.

News

Baby's first flutters

make demands, sap coherence,

telling narrative

as old as time, new as now.

Mary kept her thoughts inside.

Elizabeth's Song

That spring there was a quickening; the blossom,
saplings round the olive trees, more lush than usual,
the sheep restive, their lambs heavy.
My husband's turn; he'd waited all his life
for this one chance – called at last
behind the temple curtain to offer prayer.
We waited, waited, as all my long life I had waited.
He returned to me, silent – his tunic permeated
with the smell of incense – gesturing with smiles.

And then this pulse, a gentle thrum inside.
I'd lost hope and yet my foul mornings
(a dry retch, when raising water from the well –
water that seemed heavier and slapped
with a sound that made me retch again).
Could I believe, despite my autumn years?
Outside, springtime hummed exhaustingly with life
and more life, and inside I sat in queasy silence,
Zachariah sympathetic, but dumb.
Months passed. The sickness passed. I knew.

One afternoon as summer heat oppressed all noise
I heard dogs up the valley – roused
from their sleep – dog after dog careened and howled
and let on so. Nearer and nearer. And then a shout.
Sweet Mary! My baby somersaulted with her sound.
And all the pent-up silence of those months
broke.

I sang and sang summer praises for her new life,
her hope – song of the world to break our silence –
her song, her new life, her new song.
I sang and sang and the valley rang
with the howling dogs and the song of hope,
my news, my cousin's news, a new song
that would be sung forever.

Elizabeth's Prayer

I raise my arms to you. Beyond words,
I look up in expectation, for help.
You can intervene. I cannot
know what I need, let alone want;
therefore, I am silent. I can speak only
through gesture. Here are my arms. Up.

This is a prayer I learned when the child
came to me, again and again, unaware
of my limitations, his arms requesting. A gift;
his wordless faith in my capacity to lift.

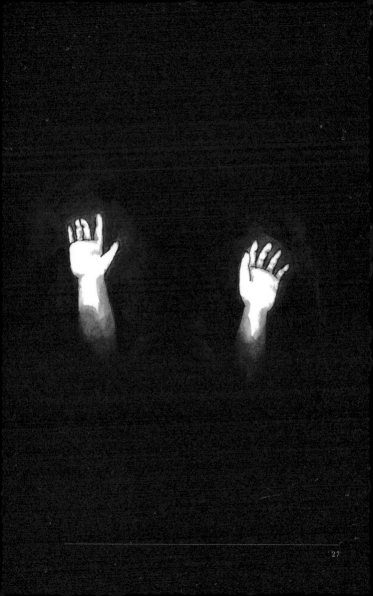

Travel

The first time, it was imperative; a Roman decree.
A census marks units of labour, projected returns
from taxes, and Caesar Augustus had remembered
the advice of an old governor. 'The first way,
dear boy, to pre-empt trouble is to bloody count 'em.
Know what's what and who you've got. Then
keep them running, this way and that'.
All were obliged to return to their family home
for assessment of assets – everyone was on the move.
That's how the girl from the wrong country town,
gave birth in the prophesied place.

Now, even if planned, our journeys are wearisome.
We fret; will they like our gifts, will there be cake,
and will the rooms will be warm? We forget
God first travelling to be with us.

Genealogy I

Do we prefer not to read these lines?

The repetitive sons of,

names unpronounceable,

yet they give location, connection.

We need to go back, go back.

The birth was not random. The story

didn't start with the baby. Lineage, yes,

a family tree, but also whispered about

before and before; foretold. A prophecy.

Genealogy II

Where to start? Matthew began,
as it were, at the beginning. Abraham.
(Credentials established.) He then traced
through the many-syllabled sons of.
There are unconventional references
to some mothers – not even Jewish.
(Motive? Every family has its shame?
A claim this story is also for Gentiles,
includes those with irregular behaviour?
Oh, not picking your nose or a failure
to change underwear. No, some
of these women had done bad things –
consensus-across-cultures bad.)
There was also perhaps in his choice
of sons of sons, a point to be made:
Joseph wasn't eligible to father a king,
an heir to the throne of David.
(Wrong family branch – and cursed.)
Only Mary was of the right line.
So, his argument goes, the baby
was God's Son – had to be.
Whatever his intent, he worked down,
past knots, through sons to the birth
at a fork in time; a place in a family tree,
from one beginning to a new beginning.

Genealogy III

Son of Adam –

The baby is human

Son of Abraham –

The baby is Jewish

Son of David –

The baby is King

Son of God –

This baby is God

Our Person-God Jewish King.

Matter of Belief

The guide from *National Geographic* suggested

it could have been a trough, rather than a manger,

where Mary laid her baby, since Bethlehem,

banked by olive and almond trees, is on an aquifer

and was built to defend water. He pontificated that

water and height, the soil and its fertility, defence,

boundaries and access remain political issues.

Trough or manger; a problem? The mystery is

in contested territory, in politically charged times

God became matter, and tiny, contained.

Cloth

She swaddled him in lengths of cloth;
rough linen cloth to dry off dew.
She lifted him up high, then held him tight.
She took his fragile form and bathed
him free of blood, her tears.
She swaddled him in lengths of cloth.
She smiled, she kissed his head
and rubbed his tiny forehead free of frowns.
She lifted him up high, then held him tight.
She brushed the fabric free of straw
and swaddled him in lengths of cloth.
She cradled him and sang
the song of his arrival.
She lifted him up high then held him tight.
She knew there was a time ahead
when he would be held high, then wrapped in white.
She swaddled him in lengths of cloth.
She lifted him up high then held him tight.

A Shepherd Reflects

We were scorned; for our rough dry bread,
the fact that we didn't know what to do with fish,
for the cloaks that spoke our business – sheep.
Oh, when it came to Passover, they
were willing to set aside their snobberies –
they paid good money for lambs. But,
ordinarily, we got barely a nod as they clip-clopped by.
We roamed – weeks at a time, searching out grazing,
ready to lob a stone at wild dogs, alert for snakes,
avoiding thickets, keeping near caves in storms.
Skilled at survival, we were despised by those
who considered themselves rather better.
The nights were hard; bitter, without women.
We lit a fire, told stories, jokes. Sometimes there was liquor.
One night as we settled, a blazing appeared.
I thought it was for a laugh – they'd set me up,
but then the terror set in. All of us. Like a weird summons
from another world – where was the source of the noise –
the focus? We stumbled in the light. And yet the sheep slept.
Then a big voice. A booming instruction. We argued.
Who had the best idea? Should we scamper off?
Then a roar of voices; a glory of sound that went beyond
head space and left us breathless, doubt crammed out.

We left Sam to watch the sheep and ran
and ran. Into town, looking in every doorway, flight of steps.
We found the baby! A young pair. Not in a nice inn,
but poor, like us, maybe even worse.
And a story enough to last all our lives
told to anyone who asked and who would listen.
And those who passed by – clip clop clip clop –
or who drove past in chariots hadn't even seen.

Passers-by

In times of occupation

talk's driven underground,

trust compromised.

A baby can be cover

but the pair out back

probably looked harmless,

their night-time visitors

chaotic; unlikely rebels.

They must have attracted

sly looks, a few silent

but quizzical shrugs.

Kindness, too, perhaps.

What Anna Saw

At that time, I was one of a few;
prophets are valued when times are febrile,
the kings quixotic. One never knew.
There were deals and rumours of deals.
I kept out of it: confined my days to the temple.
The rhythm of prayer and fast days
had helped me through my widow grief,
and I stayed there – I had nothing to lose
and it meant less time at my in-laws' house.
I watched: boys in groups with their Rabbi,
trying not to cough or laugh at the spicy air,
the irony tang of butchered meat; the deliveries
of firewood and the finest nards; the money changers
with their patter, charming the unwary;
the man with lambs. I knew them all.
I dealt in small stuff – dreams of an inherited field,
rights of way, the future of a tree at harvest.
I longed for big pronouncements; of when the Romans
would be broken by their own arrangements,
or when Israel would at last be free,
but my predictions, like most prophets' at that time
remained local, concerned the very slow.
I do not know why, after a life of small things

I got to see him – the salvation of Israel –
his parents edging through the gate
for the first born, counting their money
to buy the least ostentatious sacrifice.
The doves fluttered before the axe fell.
The child sensed the unfamiliar air,
the tension of the ceremonial, and mewled.
I held him, soothed his tiny frame
and knew the largest vision ever.

Simeon's Story

It was one thing the Romans couldn't fault;
the collection of domestic firewood.
It became a habit, after the day's trading and
temple prayers; once or twice a week,
beyond the city walls, I'd pick up gnarly olive logs,
twigs and pine cones for kindling, trail them home.
Soldiers at the gates never saw me as a threat;
a dried-out stick of a man with his basket.
Each time I passed them I would pray
for our tortured, occupied Israel, and think
of the promise; the voice that said I would see
the liberator before I died.
I had waited; seen stack after stack
burnt for a thousand winter fires,
seen new vines sprawl over the terrace
cut back and regrow year after year.
Yesterday – was it Spirit or a whim?
I went early to the temple – saw
two country folks doing the right thing
with doves – gratitude, as the custom is,

for their first-born boy-child.
And I reached out – to the young shoot –
the root of Jesse – come to us at last.
I held the child; his parents diffident
at my delight. Now I need no more
meditative lifting of firewood
and no more fires – I can depart this earth
content. For I have seen the promise.
Green sapling of hope – the living wood.

Star of Bethlehem

A conjunction of planets:
a comet; a nova (birth of
a new star), or a miracle
(without explanation)?
Oblivious, the quilters
sense the need for joy
in their choice of colours, know
effort should focus more
on effect than on perfect points;
a burst of visual delight.
They choose this pattern,
cut cloth, stitch and patch
this many-sided star,
and sense its significance,
the ancient story.
Learned men. Interpreters
of skies. The decision
to trust their knowledge,
traverse deserts, hopeful,
follow what they could see,
follow the foretold.

Herod

It was the Roman way – a new-born,
slithery, on the floor, bloody –

could be picked up, made safe. Or not.
Neonaticide; the father's right.

Herod, who had allowed some sons to live,
later had them killed – wives, too. A threat.

It's therefore no surprise scribes note
his times featured weeping mothers.

His survival depended on the people's fear –
of his grandiose buildings, his bodyguards and spies.

(That, and his loyalty to Rome. The Senate styled
him 'King' to keep him aligned.)

Then these sultry Persian visitors, searching,
using his title, 'King of the Jews'. For a child?

Blind to his lies, they fled. They'd dreamed of him.
Bad dreams they knew they had to heed.

The Three Gifts

They were from the east.
Arabian or Persian –
Zoroastrian, sorcerers,
astrologers, or kings.
They had read the signs;
believed their interpretation
enough to invest hope
in a foreign child.
Nor was this trio of gifts
Jewish; the givers were, after all,
from the east, so they brought
their exotic, temple gifts.
The story goes that the three
materials were a test.
Which would the recipient choose;
was he a healer, priest or king?
This child, or Mary on his behalf,
selected all three.
And the giving continues and
we can give only what is ours
within and from our time
and he continues to make holy
our pagan gifts.

Myrrh

Myrrh is a tree's weepings;
the bark is cut and sap rises,
drips. Then the desert air
dries and solidifies the drops.
The amber-coloured tears
are gathered and sold.
We can only guess its relative
worth; more potent and costly,
we are assured, than frankincense.
Nor do we know how the men
transported the myrrh. A cedar box
seems appropriate, but we do not
know what quantity they carried.
We possess one material fact;
the stuff has analgesic properties –
the ailments of early motherhood
are salved by its application –
but whether internal or external,
and in what combinations –
we do not know the ancients' formulary.
This scented gift, perhaps a remedy,
echoes to future memories:
a balm comforting the psalmists;
a presence at the court of Israel;
the healer given a sign of healing;
a tree, more than thirty years on,
this mother, or other women, weeping
at the hanging man, pulling his lips away,
to refuse myrrh mixed with sour wine.

Frankincense

The child –

and scholars agree

he was, by this visit,

a child – sat up,

and sneezed at the

essence of resins

that is frankincense,

presented to him,

oblivious to its

priestly resonances.

The Third Gift

It is enough to recognize
the metaphor of myrrh and frankincense.
What is the meaning of this third gift?

Gold: perhaps rough nuggets
panned for, by expert hands
in rivers swift with snow-melt,
or excavated ore, smelted, and shaped
to a pour of glittering coins.

Not paper, inscribed 'pay the bearer',
derivatives, options, an 'I owe you',
not shares, a stake, or a promise,
but the substance of worth itself.
The means to live wrapped
in a leather pouch, or a silk purse,
one transaction away from food.

This gift showed: the givers' wisdom,
for metaphor will not buy bread;
the practical can be a form of prophesy
(the flight to Egypt would cost them dear);
the age-old link between
worship and love and love and
the working of a precious ore;
the ancient truth
that gold will follow hope.

Art

Did he come down to be mocked up
in plaster of Paris, or pale wood
painted with vermilion wounds,
paraded through streets each fiesta?
Did he come down to be a statue
handled by men in white gloves,
gently winched onto a plinth?
Did he come down to model
for Raphael or Leonardo;
on a beatific Mary's lap?
Yes, he came down, for all our poor
attempts to represent what we sense,
or consider beautiful and in good taste;
he came down and has compassion
on our worst art, and on our best.

Narrative II

The story of his birth – how should it be framed? Mere arrival? There is little detail; a back room, limited resources.

The witnesses. They must be recognized: some illiterate; sophisticates from a different tradition; those who'd looked out for this child for years. These are the only ones on record. Others must have passed by.

Then the necessary commentary on historical context. Who knows when 'significance' enters the world? It's only with hindsight we recognize that yes, this birth divides time. Or having privileged information, perhaps from prophets or seers or angels, confirms this is a hinge moment.

There are the mysteries of angels, prophecies, new songs, strange dreams and journeys at night.

The last week of his life, everything changed. And it changed everything. But between his beginning and those last days? Before his 'doing for'? Before the water into wine, the parables, the crowds? Before the end of his human life?

There is a story of his parents losing him, an older child. He stayed on, absorbed, in the temple, his parents assuming he was with others returning home. He wasn't. For three days he was missing. They found him, still in the temple.

Another writer observes, 'The child grew and became strong'. This is what every parent would wish. Then there is an additional observation, 'He was filled with wisdom, and the grace of God was upon him'.

His birth was the beginning of an undocumented time; most of a human life. He was immersed in the ordinary, negotiating the stuff of life, bending to God. This is Immanuel. Him 'being with'. Then. Now. Always.

Muddy
Pearl